~A BINGO BOOK~

Alaska Bingo Book

COMPLETE BINGO GAME IN A BOOK

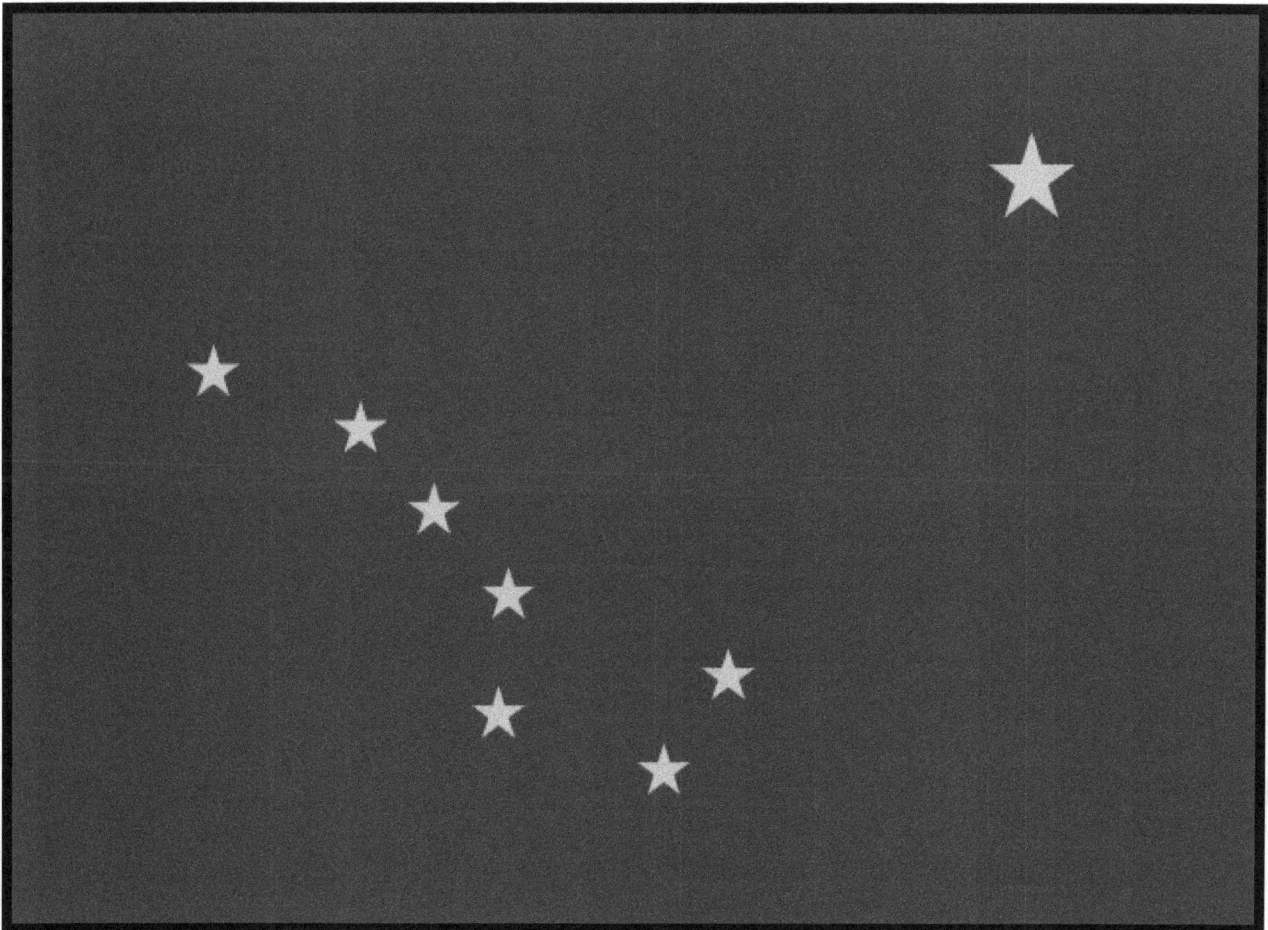

Written By Rebecca Stark
Educational Books 'n' Bingo

ISBN 978-0-87386-495-4

Educational Books 'n' Bingo

Printed in the U.S.A.

DIRECTIONS

INCLUDED:

List of Terms

Templates for Additional Terms and Clues

2 Clues per Term

30 Unique Bingo Cards

Markers

1. **Either cut apart the book or make copies of ALL the sheets. You might want to make an extra copy of the clue sheets to use for introduction and review. Keep the sheets in an envelope for easy reuse.**

2. Cut apart the call cards with terms and clues.

3. Pass out one bingo card per student. There are enough for a class of 30.

4. Pass out markers. You may cut apart the markers included in this book or use any other small items of your choice.

5. Decide whether or not you will require the entire card to be filled. Requiring the entire card to be filled provides a better review. However, if you have a short time to fill, you may prefer to have them do the just the border or some other format. Tell the class before you begin what is required.

6. There are 50 terms. Read the list before you begin. If there are any terms that have not been covered in class, you may want to read to the students the term and clues before you begin.

7. There is a blank space in the middle of each card. You can instruct the students to use it as a free space or you can write in answers to cover terms not included. Of course, in this case you would create your own clues. (Templates provided.)

8. Shuffle the cards and place them in a pile. Two or three clues are provided for each term. If you plan to play the game with the same group more than once, you might want to choose a different clue for each game. If not, you may choose to use more than one clue.

9. Be sure to keep the cards you have used for the present game in a separate pile. When a student calls, "Bingo," he or she will have to verify that the correct answers are on his or her card AND that the markers were placed in response to the proper questions. Pull out the cards that are on the student's card keeping them in the order they were used in the game. Read each clue as it was given and ask the student to identify the correct answer from his or her card.

10. If the student has the correct answers on the card AND has shown that they were marked in response to the *correct questions,* then that student is the winner and the game is over. If the student does not have the correct answers on the card OR he or she marked the answers in response to *the wrong questions,* then the game continues until there is a proper winner.

11. If you want to play again, reshuffle the cards and begin again.

Have fun!

TERMS

Alaska Territory

Anchorage

Arctic Coastal Plain

Bering Sea

Bordered

Boroughs

Bowhead Whale

Central Uplands and Lowlands

Denali

Dog Mushing

Executive Branch

Fairbanks

Fishing

Flag

Forget-Me-Not

Glacier

Gold

Gulf of Alaska

Iditarod

Industry (-ies)

Inside Passage

Jade

Judicial Branch

Juneau

Ketchikan

King Salmon

Lake(s)

Legislative Branch

Malamute

Moose

Motto

Mount McKinley

Native Alaskans

Nickname

Oil

Pacific Mountain System

Peninsula(s)

River(s)X

Rocky Mountain System

Seal

Sitka

Sitka Spruce

Willow Ptarmigan

William H. Seward

Song

Tourism

Tundra

Union

Volcanoes

Woolly Mammoth

Additional Terms

Choose as many additional terms as you would like and write them in the squares. Repeat each as desired.
Cut out the squares and randomly distribute them to the class.
Instruct the students to place their square on the center space of their card.

Alaska Bingo

Clues for Additional Terms

Write three clues for each of your additional terms.

_____	_____
1.	1.
2.	2.
3.	3.
_____	_____
1.	1.
2.	2.
3.	3.
_____	_____
1.	1.
2.	2.
3.	3.

Alaska Bingo

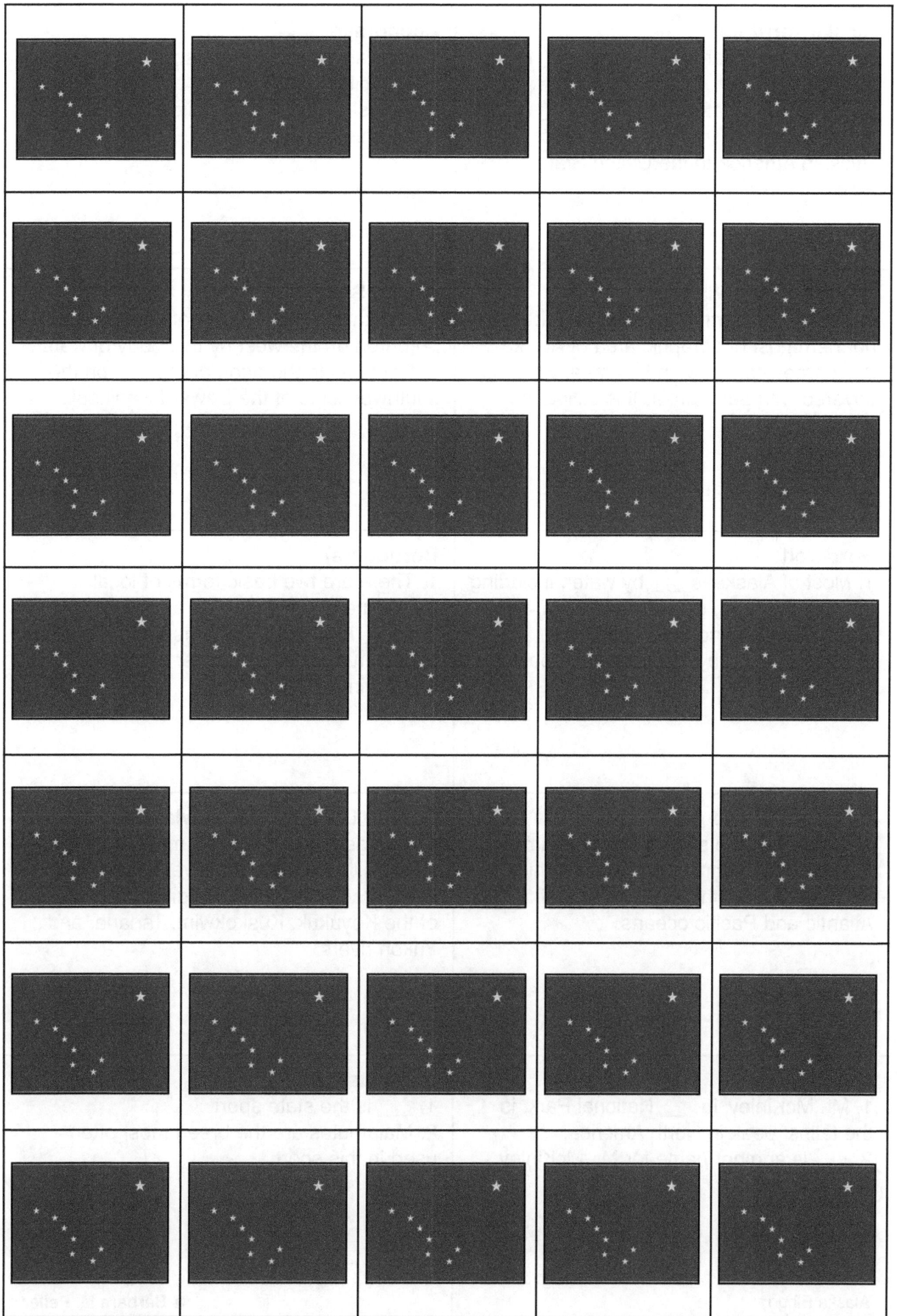

Alaska Territory 1. The United States purchased ___ in 1867. 2. The United States purchased ___ under the terms of the Treaty of Cession of Russian America to the United States.	**Anchorage** 1. With almost 300,000 residents, ___ is the largest city. 2. Almost half of all the residents in Alaska live in this city.
Arctic Coastal Plain 1. The ___ is north of the Rockies. It is the northernmost geographic area of Alaska. 2. No trees can grow in this area, which is covered with permafrost. It is called the tundra.	**Bering Sea** 1. Alaska has 6,640 miles of coastline. It is bordered on the west by this body of water. 2. Nome is on the edge of the ___ on the southwest side of the Seward Peninsula.
Bordered 1. Most of Alaska is ___ by water, including the Arctic Ocean, the Gulf of Alaska, the Pacific Ocean, and the Bering Sea. 2. Alaska is ___ by Canada to the east and south.	**Borough(s)** 1. There are two basic forms of local government in Alaska: city and ___. 2. A ___ is similar to what is referred to as a county in most other states. Alaska is divided into 16 ___.
Bowhead Whale 1. The ___ is the state marine mammal. 2. This large marine mammal with thick blubber inhabits the Arctic waters of the Atlantic and Pacific oceans.	**Central Uplands and Lowlands** 1. This geographic area is marked by low, rolling hills and swampy river valleys. 2. River valleys in this region include those of the Koyukuk, Kuskokwim, Tanana, and Yukon rivers.
Denali 1. Mt. McKinley, in ___ National Park, is the tallest peak in North America. 2. ___ is another name for Mt. McKinley.	**Dog Mushing** 1. ___ is the state sport. 2. Malamutes are the breed most often used in this sport.

Alaska Bingo

Executive Branch	Fairbanks
1. The governor and lieutenant governor are part of the ___. 2. The present-day governor is [fill in]. The governor is head of the ___ and appoints the heads of the state departments and many other officials.	1. ___ is the second largest city in Alaska. It is in the interior part of Alaska. 2. ___ is in the central Tanana Valley. It is situated on the Chena River.
Fishing 1. Because of its vast coastline, ___ is a very important industry. 2. The most important commercial ___ ports are at Kodiak and Unalaska/Dutch Harbor. Cod, flounder, pollock, rockfish, sablefish, salmon, and smelt are of great importance.	**Flag** 1. The Alaska state ___ has a field of blue. 2. The North Star and the Big Dipper are on the state ___.
Forget-Me-Not 1. The wild native Alpine ___ is the state flower and floral emblem. 2. The wild native Alpine ___ is one of the few species with true blue flowers. They grow well in the open, rocky places high in the mountains.	**Glacier** 1. A large mass of ice moving slowly through a valley or spreading outward from a center is a ___. 2. Bering ___ is the longest one in North America. Malaspina ___ in southeastern Alaska is the largest piedmont ___ in the world.
Gold 1. The state mineral is ___. 2. The ___ Rush of 1898 lured thousands of people to Alaska. Mining towns or gateways included Fairbanks, Juneau, and Skagway.	**Gulf of Alaska** 1. Alaska's southern borders are the ___ and the Pacific Ocean. 2. Alaska's largest glaciers, the Malaspina Glacier and Bering Glacier, flow out onto the coastal plain along the ___.
Iditarod 1. The ___ is the largest and most famous sled-dog race in the world. 2. The ___ covers more than 1,150 miles, from Anchorage to Nome. The Yukon Quest is a 1,000-mile race run between Whitehorse, Yukon, and Fairbanks, Alaska.	**Industry (-ies)** 1. Major industries include oil and gas, commercial fishing, mining, and timber. 2. Tourism is also an important ___. More than one million people visit the state each year.

Alaska Bingo

© Barbara M. Peller

Inside Passage
1. Many cruise ships make their way through the islands of the ___.
2. Towns of Alaska's ___ include Juneau, Ketchikan, Sitka, Skagway, and Haines.

Jade
1. ___ is the state gem.
2. ___ is a popular medium for Alaskan carvers.

Judicial Branch
1. The ___ consists of the Alaska Court System, the Alaska Judicial Council and the Alaska Commission on Judicial Conduct.
2. The chief justice of the Alaska Supreme Court is the administrative head of the Alaska Court System, or ___.

Juneau
1. ___ is the capital of Alaska.
2. Mendenhall Glacier is one of ___'s most popular attractions.

Ketchikan
1. ___ is built on the site of a former Tlingit fishing camp. It is sometimes called "The Salmon Capital of the World."
2. ___ is the wettest city in the U.S. The average annual rainfall is 162 inches.

King Salmon
1. ___, or chinook, is the state fish.
2. The ___ is native to the Pacific coast of North America and is the largest of all Pacific salmon.

Lake(s)
1. Iliamna, Aleknagik, Becharof, Clark, and Minchumina are ___ in Alaska. Iliamna is America's second largest freshwater one.
2. Alaska has over 3 million ___ that are more than 20 acres in size. About 3,000 of these bodies of water are named.

Legislative Branch
1. The ___ makes the the laws and raises and distributes the money necessary to run the state government.
2. The ___is composed of two bodies, the House of Representatives and the Senate.

Malamute
1. The state dog is the Alaskan ___.
2. The Alaskan ___ is the most popular breed for dog sledding, or mushing.

Moose
1. The ___ is the state land mammal.
2. ___ are the largest member of the deer family, and the Alaskan ___ is the largest of all.

Alaska Bingo

Motto 1. The state ___ is "North to the Future." 2. The state ___ is meant to represent Alaska as a land of promise.	**Mount McKinley** 1. At 20,320 feet, ___, or Denali, is the highest point in the United States. 2. ___, in Denali National Park, is the tallest peak in North America.
Native Alaskans 1. There are five distinct groups of ___: Aleut; Athabascan; Tlingit and Haida; Inupiat, or Northern Eskimos; and Yupik, or Southern Eskimos. 2. ___ are those peoples indigenous to Alaska.	**Nickname** 1. The state ___ is called "The Last Frontier" because of its rugged landscape, harsh climate, lightly settled regions, and many opportunities. 2. Another ___ for the state is "Land of the Midnight Sun." It is called this because in some areas of the state the sun shines almost 24 hours a day during the summer.
Oil 1. ___ is the most important mined product. 2. ___ provides about 95 percent of Alaska's mining income.	**Pacific Mountain System** 1. The Saint Elias Mountain Range is a subgroup of the ___. 2. Alaska's southern coast is part of the series of mountain ranges called the ___.
Peninsula(s) 1. The Alaska ___ separates the Pacific Ocean from Bristol Bay. The Kenai ___ is separated from the mainland by Cook Inlet and Prince William Sound. 2. Long ago the Seward ___ was part of the Bering land bridge that connected Siberia with mainland Alaska.	**River(s)** 1. The Yukon ___ is the longest in Alaska. It is the third longest in the nation after the Mississippi and the Missouri. 2. The Yukon, Kuskokwim, Colville, and Copper are among the many ___ in the state.
Rocky Mountain System 1. The ___ region of Alaska is north of the Central Uplands and Lowlands. 2. The Brooks Range and the Brooks Range foothills are part of the ___. The eastern part of this region contains glacier-made mountain peaks that are as high as 9,000 feet above sea level. Lower elevations are in the west. Alaska Bingo	**Seal** 1. A smelter, a train, ships, trees, mountains and a farmer are on Alaska's Great ___. Rays over the mountains represent the Northern Lights. 2. On the outer circle of the Great ___ are two images: a seal and a fish. They show the importance of fishing and wildlife to Alaska's economy. © **Barbara M. Peller**

Sitka
1. The Russian Orthodox Cathedral of St. Michael in ___ is listed in the National Register of Historic Places.
2. ___was the site of the ceremony during which the Russian flag was lowered and the United States flag raised after Alaska was purchased by the United States in 1867.

Sitka Spruce
1. The ___ is the state tree.
2. The ___ is said to be the most valuable tree species in Alaska. It is the tallest conifer in the world.

Willow Ptarmigan
1. The ___ is the state bird.
2. In the summer the ___ is brown; in the winter its feathers turn white.

William H. Seward
1. As President Johnson's secretary of state, he negotiated the 1867 purchase of Alaska from Russia.
2. His purchase of Alaska for the United States was ridiculed by many.

Song
1. "Alaska's Flag," written by Marie Drake, is the state ___.
2. The first line of the state ___ is "Eight stars of gold on a field of blue."

Tourism
1. ___ is a major sector of Alaska's economy. The state attracts over one million visitors each year.
2. Growth in cruise ship travel is a main reason for the increase of ___ in Alaska.

Tundra
1. The ___ is the coldest, harshest biome. It is treeless.
2. The ___ has a layer of permanently frozen soil, called permafrost. The northernmost geographic area of Alaska is in this biome.

Union
1. On January 3, 1959, Alaska became the 49th state in the ___.
2. Alaska covers 656,425 square miles, making it the largest state in the ___. It is more than twice the size of Texas, the second largest state.

Volcanoes
1. About 90 of Alaska's ___ have been active within the last 10,000 years, and more than 50 have been active since about 1760, when written records of the eruptions began.
2. Most of Alaska's ___ are located along the 1,550-mile-long Aleutian Arc, which forms the northern portion of the Pacific "Ring of Fire."

Woolly Mammoth
1. The ___ is the state fossil.
2. These giant grass-eaters of the Ice Age tundra weighed about 6 to 8 tons.

Alaska Bingo

Alaska Bingo

River(s)	Alaska Territory	Arctic Coastal Plain	Iditarod	Bordered
Gold	Anchorage	Union	Moose	Sitka
Tundra	Malamute		Oil	Volcanoes
Tourism	Seal	Song	Legislative Branch	Mount McKinley
Nickname	Jade	Flag	Willow Ptarmigan	Ketchikan

Alaska Bingo

Tourism	Tundra	Juneau	Rocky Mountain System	Lake(s)
Mount McKinley	Forget-Me-Not	Central Uplands and Lowlands	Seal	Native Alaskans
Dog Mushing	Jade		Judicial Branch	Song
Pacific Mountain System	Peninsula(s)	Malamute	Woolly Mammoth	Bordered
Sitka	Union	Flag	Gold	Willow Ptarmigan

Alaska Bingo: Card No. 2

Alaska Bingo

Jade	Song	Forget-Me-Not	Legislative Branch	Tundra
Mount McKinley	Anchorage	Denali	Alaska Territory	Inside Passage
Seal	Union		Native Alaskans	Bering Sea
Malamute	Dog Mushing	Nickname	Pacific Mountain System	Juneau
Willow Ptarmigan	Executive Branch	Flag	Woolly Mammoth	Lake(s)

Alaska Bingo

Malamute	Native Alaskans	Arctic Coastal Plain	Executive Branch	Lake(s)
Motto	Bowhead Whale	Alaska Territory	Rocky Mountain System	Tundra
Oil	Pacific Mountain System		Ketchikan	Iditarod
Song	Anchorage	Union	Flag	Central Uplands and Lowlands
Fairbanks	Sitka	Boroughs	Willow Ptarmigan	Volcanoes

Alaska Bingo

Sitka	Bordered	Seal	Central Uplands and Lowlands	Executive Branch
Motto	Song	Denali	Judicial Branch	Anchorage
Arctic Coastal Plain	Volcanoes		Moose	Industry (-ies)
Ketchikan	Lake(s)	River(s)	Woolly Mammoth	Fishing
Forget-Me-Not	Flag	Tundra	Malamute	Oil

Alaska Bingo: Card No. 5

Alaska Bingo

Bering Sea	Native Alaskans	Juneau	Lake(s)	Volcanoes
Legislative Branch	Seal	Fishing	Alaska Territory	Tundra
Rocky Mountain System	Fairbanks		Bowhead Whale	Judicial Branch
Flag	Nickname	Woolly Mammoth	Boroughs	Arctic Coastal Plain
Mount McKinley	Central Uplands and Lowlands	River(s)	Oil	Glacier

Alaska Bingo: Card No. 6

Alaska Bingo

River(s)	Native Alaskans	Industry (-ies)	Song	Forget-Me-Not
Mount McKinley	Lake(s)	Jade	Anchorage	Motto
Volcanoes	Iditarod		Judicial Branch	Bowhead Whale
Malamute	Pacific Mountain System	Denali	Tourism	Dog Mushing
Flag	Executive Branch	Woolly Mammoth	Boroughs	Bering Sea

Alaska Bingo

Oil	Native Alaskans	Gulf of Alaska	Legislative Branch	Bowhead Whale
Motto	Arctic Coastal Plain	Rocky Mountain System	Volcanoes	Central Uplands and Lowlands
Glacier	Executive Branch		Lake(s)	Bordered
Willow Ptarmigan	Malamute	Tourism	Fairbanks	Pacific Mountain System
Union	Flag	Boroughs	Seal	Mount McKinley

Alaska Bingo: Card No. 8

Alaska Bingo

Judicial Branch	Forget-Me-Not	Jade	Glacier	Executive Branch
Fairbanks	Lake(s)	Oil	Seal	Native Alaskans
Inside Passage	River(s)		Anchorage	Gulf of Alaska
Fishing	Bordered	Nickname	Moose	Industry (-ies)
Pacific Mountain System	Woolly Mammoth	Denali	Tourism	Ketchikan

Alaska Bingo

Tourism	Legislative Branch	Bowhead Whale	Rocky Mountain System	Glacier
Volcanoes	Central Uplands and Lowlands	Alaska Territory	Anchorage	Lake(s)
Executive Branch	Native Alaskans		Iditarod	Dog Mushing
Nickname	Ketchikan	Fishing	Woolly Mammoth	Inside Passage
Denali	Mount McKinley	Juneau	Sitka	Oil

Alaska Bingo: Card No. 10

Alaska Bingo

Bering Sea	Native Alaskans	Seal	Fishing	Mount McKinley
Gulf of Alaska	Inside Passage	Moose	Judicial Branch	Alaska Territory
Motto	Lake(s)		Juneau	Jade
Denali	Tundra	Woolly Mammoth	Executive Branch	Tourism
Fairbanks	Flag	River(s)	Boroughs	Forget-Me-Not

Alaska Bingo

Forget-Me-Not	Bordered	Inside Passage	Legislative Branch	Judicial Branch
Jade	Mount McKinley	Arctic Coastal Plain	Boroughs	Anchorage
River(s)	Industry (-ies)		Volcanoes	Rocky Mountain System
Flag	Pacific Mountain System	Lake(s)	Tourism	Motto
Native Alaskans	Gulf of Alaska	Executive Branch	Fairbanks	Central Uplands and Lowlands

Alaska Bingo: Card No. 12

Alaska Bingo

Fishing	Bordered	Bering Sea	Inside Passage	Volcanoes
Arctic Coastal Plain	Gulf of Alaska	Lake(s)	Judicial Branch	Dog Mushing
Legislative Branch	Central Uplands and Lowlands		Jade	Industry (-ies)
Oil	Woolly Mammoth	Bowhead Whale	Executive Branch	Tourism
Flag	Ketchikan	Boroughs	River(s)	Moose

Alaska Bingo

Gold	Lake(s)	Seal	Judicial Branch	Fairbanks
Central Uplands and Lowlands	River(s)	Inside Passage	Anchorage	Native Alaskans
Fishing	Iditarod		Juneau	Denali
Ketchikan	Woolly Mammoth	Executive Branch	Bowhead Whale	Bering Sea
Flag	Rocky Mountain System	Dog Mushing	Mount McKinley	Oil

Alaska Bingo

Moose	Judicial Branch	Seal	Forget-Me-Not	Legislative Branch
Bering Sea	Juneau	Alaska Territory	Arctic Coastal Plain	Fairbanks
Volcanoes	River(s)		Tundra	Native Alaskans
Flag	Inside Passage	Gulf of Alaska	Woolly Mammoth	Fishing
Mount McKinley	Pacific Mountain System	Boroughs	Glacier	Jade

Alaska Bingo: Card No. 15

Alaska Bingo

Bowhead Whale	Inside Passage	Gulf of Alaska	Glacier	Peninsula(s)
Rocky Mountain System	Dog Mushing	Industry (-ies)	Motto	Iditarod
Fishing	Bordered		Volcanoes	Jade
Malamute	Central Uplands and Lowlands	Flag	Moose	Tourism
Fairbanks	William H. Seward	Boroughs	Pacific Mountain System	Native Alaskans

Alaska Bingo: Card No. 16

Alaska Bingo

Denali	Sitka Spruce	King Salmon	Inside Passage	Gold
Moose	Fairbanks	Woolly Mammoth	Iditarod	Industry (-ies)
Judicial Branch	Oil		William H. Seward	Gulf of Alaska
Ketchikan	Mount McKinley	Tourism	Seal	Dog Mushing
Nickname	Fishing	Forget-Me-Not	Legislative Branch	Bordered

Alaska Bingo

Glacier	Executive Branch	Central Uplands and Lowlands	Fishing	Rocky Mountain System
Native Alaskans	Denali	Nickname	Volcanoes	Fairbanks
Judicial Branch	Dog Mushing		King Salmon	Arctic Coastal Plain
Bordered	Alaska Territory	Woolly Mammoth	Tourism	Juneau
William H. Seward	Inside Passage	Seal	Sitka Spruce	Bering Sea

Alaska Bingo: Card No. 18

Alaska Bingo

Volcanoes	Bering Sea	Inside Passage	Gulf of Alaska	Tourism
Moose	Legislative Branch	Native Alaskans	Forget-Me-Not	Iditarod
Sitka Spruce	Executive Branch		Anchorage	Tundra
Juneau	William H. Seward	Nickname	Pacific Mountain System	King Salmon
Arctic Coastal Plain	Peninsula(s)	Mount McKinley	Oil	Boroughs

Alaska Bingo

Gold	Sitka Spruce	Legislative Branch	Inside Passage	Boroughs
Central Uplands and Lowlands	Jade	Motto	Nickname	Rocky Mountain System
Bordered	Industry (-ies)		Malamute	Alaska Territory
Sitka	Union	Willow Ptarmigan	Pacific Mountain System	William H. Seward
Song	Oil	Peninsula(s)	Tourism	King Salmon

Alaska Bingo

Moose	Bering Sea	Motto	Inside Passage	Sitka
Bordered	King Salmon	Bowhead Whale	Gulf of Alaska	River(s)
Dog Mushing	Mount McKinley		Sitka Spruce	Seal
Nickname	Forget-Me-Not	William H. Seward	Ketchikan	Oil
Malamute	Peninsula(s)	Boroughs	Denali	Pacific Mountain System

Alaska Bingo: Card No. 21

Alaska Bingo

Glacier	Juneau	King Salmon	Arctic Coastal Plain	Fishing
Rocky Mountain System	Legislative Branch	Tundra	Gulf of Alaska	Anchorage
Central Uplands and Lowlands	Iditarod		River(s)	Industry (-ies)
William H. Seward	Ketchikan	Pacific Mountain System	Alaska Territory	Motto
Peninsula(s)	Denali	Sitka Spruce	Dog Mushing	Oil

Alaska Bingo

Bowhead Whale	Sitka Spruce	Forget-Me-Not	Arctic Coastal Plain	Boroughs
Bering Sea	Gold	Mount McKinley	Moose	Alaska Territory
Juneau	Fishing		Willow Ptarmigan	River(s)
Dog Mushing	Peninsula(s)	William H. Seward	Denali	Pacific Mountain System
Sitka	Union	Oil	Nickname	King Salmon

Alaska Bingo

Bowhead Whale	Oil	Gold	Sitka Spruce	Gulf of Alaska
King Salmon	Boroughs	Motto	Rocky Mountain System	River(s)
Industry (-ies)	Glacier		Fishing	Dog Mushing
Sitka	Willow Ptarmigan	William H. Seward	Denali	Bordered
Song	Malamute	Peninsula(s)	Legislative Branch	Union

Alaska Bingo: Card No. 24

Alaska Bingo

Malamute	Motto	Sitka Spruce	Seal	King Salmon
Alaska Territory	Bordered	Moose	Bowhead Whale	Anchorage
Ketchikan	Gulf of Alaska		Willow Ptarmigan	William H. Seward
Tundra	Sitka	Union	Peninsula(s)	Iditarod
Boroughs	Gold	Central Uplands and Lowlands	Fairbanks	Song

Alaska Bingo

King Salmon	Sitka Spruce	Juneau	Rocky Mountain System	Glacier
Nickname	Legislative Branch	Gulf of Alaska	Gold	Bowhead Whale
Ketchikan	Willow Ptarmigan		Iditarod	Malamute
Denali	Arctic Coastal Plain	Sitka	Peninsula(s)	William H. Seward
Industry (-ies)	Fairbanks	Seal	Union	Song

Alaska Bingo: Card No. 26

Alaska Bingo

Juneau	Central Uplands and Lowlands	Sitka Spruce	Gold	Jade
Sitka	Willow Ptarmigan	Moose	William H. Seward	Anchorage
Woolly Mammoth	Union		Peninsula(s)	Malamute
Glacier	Bering Sea	Motto	Song	Alaska Territory
Fairbanks	Iditarod	King Salmon	Tundra	Industry (-ies)

Alaska Bingo

Juneau	Gold	Tundra	Sitka Spruce	Bowhead Whale
Jade	King Salmon	Willow Ptarmigan	Rocky Mountain System	Iditarod
Union	Dog Mushing		Industry (-ies)	Nickname
Tourism	Glacier	Mount McKinley	Peninsula(s)	William H. Seward
Arctic Coastal Plain	Judicial Branch	Fairbanks	Song	Sitka

Alaska Bingo

King Salmon	Gold	Glacier	Moose	Judicial Branch
Pacific Mountain System	Nickname	Motto	Industry (-ies)	Tundra
Ketchikan	Willow Ptarmigan		Anchorage	Sitka Spruce
Jade	Sitka	Lake(s)	Peninsula(s)	William H. Seward
Bowhead Whale	Gulf of Alaska	Song	Bering Sea	Union

Alaska Bingo

Executive Branch	Sitka Spruce	Rocky Mountain System	Judicial Branch	William H. Seward
Alaska Territory	Gold	Juneau	Iditarod	Anchorage
Ketchikan	Fishing		Industry (-ies)	Motto
Song	Bering Sea	Arctic Coastal Plain	Peninsula(s)	Willow Ptarmigan
Sitka	Volcanoes	Union	King Salmon	Tundra